Dream Salvage

For Kwm,
In language,
Jonathan
27.VI.2017
Edmonton

Dream Salvage

by

Jonathan Locke Hart

BuschekBooks

National Library of Canada Cataloguing in Publication Data

Hart, Jonathan Locke, 1956-
   Dream salvage / by Jonathan Locke Hart.

Poems.
ISBN 1-894543-15-7

      I. Title.

PS8565.A6656D745 2003   C811'.6   C2003-904801-2

The cover background is based on a plasma fractal generated by
John Buschek.

Printed in Canada by Hignell Book Printing, Winnipeg, Manitoba.

BuschekBooks gratefully acknowledges the support of the Canada
Council for the Arts and the Ontario Arts Council for its publishing
program.

BuschekBooks
P.O. Box 74053, 5 Beechwood Avenue
Ottawa, Ontario K1M 2H9
Canada
Email: buschek.books@sympatico.ca

For Julia and James

But in a Fixion, in a dreame of Passion

Hamlet

'Tis farre off:
And rather like a dreame, then an assurance
That my remembrance warrants

Miranda

Acknowledgements

To the Muse and muses. Thank you to John Buschek for making substance of this dream and the series of poetic fictions of which it is a part. More thanks to friends, family, teachers, students, editors, poets and writers for being there and making a difference along the way; to E.D. Blodgett, poet and friend, and others who have transfigured and translated my poetry, most especially, Nicole Mallet; to my audiences and readers, who amidst the demands and distractions of this bustling world took or will take some time with these words and this stuff of dreams; to my parents, Jean and George, who themselves were touched by poetry and met in a play; to my wife, Mary, who has made so much possible and whose musings have shaped a world of their own; to James and Julia, our twins, to whom this book is dedicated in particular, whose lives and dreams have transformed mine, who might understand best what a dialogue might sound like between Hamlet and Miranda and who can salvage from putative spaces the tomorrow of remembrance of things past, whether cultivated or wild, in the green of forest or pasture, in the city, the sea or the liminal, in the gap between fiction and dream, word and world.

Table of Contents

one

trying to salvage dreams from the tear
of breath
                the garment
shed by day

making sense of uncharted worlds
deep in blood and skull

dreams falling between brain and mind
played out in the turning body.

1

In fallen streams
grass abounds

his head
a beacon

the coin
he held

the steed
with the golden

bridle turn
with the sun

the hills cold
the rain and

dew washing
the fruit

flush on the mouths
of the dead.

2

The moon on the brook
was a bird that was gone

the storm had fled
a horse from the barn

the glaze of autumn
was on the black water

her silk made me crazy
on the front afar

and she far from breath
in this dust and dread

the land

the dream of her tongue
a mortal wisp.

3

The wind is a mast
she sleeps for the stars

the taxes are blood
the dog moans

tiger bones heap up
in mythology

and you in the mansion
of your dream

weigh youth
petals falling

the moon a pain
suspended

on the water
once more.

4

her hair blond as a barbarian

he delved for salmon
in a stream, white-water

swirling.

       she heard about the east
from centurions at the bounds

of love and empire.

5

they spin and cut
by another river

the taste of leaves on their tongues.

6

she played music in the snow
consoled the man by the window

his glory had fled
like geese from winter

he stole this bride from his son

he gave his empire to the son
of a Turkish sorceress

she touched by
Morgan on Cornish cliffs

in the death of the upstart

the crows began to circle
the warlords rose up

and a eunuch strangled her
by a pear tree

the old man wept in his heart
his tears dew from her lips

the whisper of her song
the snow of peach-blossoms.

7

birds covering the infant with wings

millet black, pink, white
plums laid out in shallow baskets

he carries feathers in his hand
like a song cycle for the birth

of a nation.

she gave him a red flute
and he blushed like Mars

in the night sky. mulberry and willow
haunt the fire

the rising sun soon bakes to waste the fields
our wagons are hearses.

8

he built a bridge across the Rhine
the rebellion still fresh in his mind

they marched through
the forest, pitched camp
amid the earthworks

they took the long route
though the dark wood.

                    the sickness
of war was in their brains

in the stench
of woman and child in heaps

they had been making death-camps
since the beginning

no one stopped to ask
the temple of Tanfana lay in ruins

the Germans on the verge of dream
died like massacred bison

half-way across the world

blood smattered faces
crazed trophies.

two

the cold sweat of history
filling my sheets

the confusion of time
misplaced

like confidence. why these
fragments haunt

why these ancient wars
in the ruin of an after-time?

these wounds are
my embarrassment, the excuse

invented after, the wind
at my back.

9

flute, stone, drum

the heir at the harvest moon
will turn

       earth, clay, lime
protect the dead.

                              behold
the steam rising the dusk

that might
bring a stranger

beyond the gate.

10

pear-tree spindles
a spider hangs

the flowers by the marsh
are white

                    the juice
over-ripe

killing what is here and now.

11

the republicans were long dead
pax and bread and empire entombed

the Germans guarded
against mutiny on the frontiers

but they lost nerve
                    the winter came

the rain would not cease

the tents
sopped the blood

and the grand-daughter
of the dead emperor

fled pregnant,

her husband
crossed the Rhine

to die
in a dark wood.

12

the duke dreamt that an ogre
was pursuing him because he had killed
his grandsons. the sorcerer said

the dream meant the duke would die
before the new grain, but he was alive
at harvest, so, being a duke,

he put the wizard to death. but his stomach
began to swell and, as he sought relief,
he fell down the hole and died.

a servant to the duke dreamt that he had carried
the duke to heaven, so he was assigned to bear
him out of the hole. they executed this man

so he could bear his load and get all the way
to heaven, and live his dream, as all people
desire, before the break of day.

13

he had his soldiers slaughter
                    burn
drive

between Rhine and Elbe they rose up
the gibbets and pits for the Roman prisoners

lined the marshes six years after.

                    the Cherusci
were big and thrust their lances far
at night

the Romans murmured by their fires
that smouldered and hissed in the damp.

the general dreamt that Varus, lost in the last
war, rose out of the morass,

mantled in blood.

                    the Germans began to loot
soon dead from greed

                         they rushed
over parapet

the smell of the dead on the wind.

14

snow foams
hearts grieve
dragons beat

the waves, feast
on the whispers
of ladies gazing

on the sedge.
you threw your ring
into the bay.

15

zither and bell
you ride the thunder

beat the drum
the elmwood bows
below

the maidens
sing until the end of time.

16

the soldier whose name was Germany
heard his men call

he dreamt Augusta gave him a new robe
the old one stained with sacrifice.

the Germans are large but flee when hurt.

                              death is better
than chains to their men who flee

with oars and winds

                        the Germans hung
in trees shot through with arrows, swam

the Weser stabbed with javelins—the riverbanks
collapsed—and were carried away

with the current
the mass of fugitives

lay massacred in heaps—old, wet boots
red under the sun.

17

I would fade as you fade
would drink as you do the rain.

18

no prisoners, Germanicus said,
and the huge swift Germans fell

heaped and strewn
between the Rhine and Elbe.

three

why should anyone care
about people long past

ancestors or not?
the dead are forgotten

stray evidence
supports to myth

and theory. why
do I make a saga

of sleep?

19

hailstorm, squall scattered a thousand ships
the savage North Sea on one side, the enemy

coast on another.

                 the gale rose
the waters swelled

                 horses, arms, baggage
jettisoned.

                 the soldiers
ate the horses that washed up.

                         When
the tides turned and the sea calmed

Germanicus had to ransom some
from as far as Britain.

20

the ship-wrecked thought
they had seen sea-monsters

as if they were in a new world
amid the spawn of Roman-German dead.

21

the emperor called Germanicus home
before another year might bring him
full victory

                             kings and warriors
wrestled words
in the shadow of Mars amid the groves

olives and plots sprung like corpses
from field and garden.

22

       he walked
to the Lyceum and washed

and spent the day as he might
any other, and in the evening

returned home to his bed.

23

the red ants were as huge
as elephants

       the nine-headed man
and jackals might keep you from

heaven

      come back to the quiet
of home

the catalogue of food
beasts and fowl stewed, fried, braised, seethed

the girls play their music drunk with wine
the dancers will not be denied

the king hunts by the marsh

by the river the soul
has not been seen for some time.

24

but Achilles did not know
that Patroklos was dead

                          under
the walls of Troy.

                    who wanted
then to go back to the hollow ships?

the sea
as dark as wine and blood

beat against the black earth
on the margin.

they piled the breaker of horses
in a grave-barrow: then his enemies feasted

in his father's house.

25

                    the wind
flies through pine and cedar—

the thunder shakes rocks and doors
has no class bias.

26

the weary oxen draw the wagons
the sacred dragons hide deep

in the tides. the unicorn is
neither dog nor ram.

                              the whale lies
stranded in the shoal

food for ants and crickets
and we for worms.

27

wed your vines
to your elms

the glades of Arcadia
taste the fragrance

the ice melts

and the plough
begins to furrow.

28

when the barbarians took him
he became the chief's slave

but the chief grew fond of him
and fed him well

he tried to escape
and was sold further south

another chief nailed boards to his feet
and put him in a cell at night

he dreamt images of pines and catalpas
by the graves of his family,

the man
he had written of his capture

had sold everything to keep
away this ghost

to haunt the barbarians
the prisoner knew nothing of the changes

when the men came and pulled
the nails from his feet.

four

exhausted by wakelessness
children sleep-walking

upending my sleep
I cannot read the signs

and try to drive out
images of war

the wind in blood
but am left to fend

my body broken
the accident of symbols

too immediate to dismiss
as unreal.

29

for the maintenance
of power, ruin being

not worth much to princes
and, let me assure you,

that I wear the robes of state
that I had to leave, as I write

but will go naked
from this world.

30

he passed the garden

of the sun, came to the great
mountains, where scorpions,

man-dragons, stood guard.
he searched for his friend

in death
she sits by the sea in a garden

holding a golden bowl, she
the maker of wine

why are you seeking the wind?
she said

he persisted
and she sent him down in the woods

the ferryman looked up from his boat.

and this was a world of repeated questions
and answers he had heard before

now in the form of secrets.

31

the maple is supple

the oriole song insists
the wind is a hand

a blossom drifts

on the dark calm.

32

dace, bream,
salmon shimmer

dance, flap
twist in the sun

cranes, grebes, gadwalls,
cormorants flock, swoop,

settle on the waters
the weeds a shelter.

33

fairies sun themselves under eaves
immortals eat in the towers

loquats, tamarinds, damsons scent the air
the women laugh in the shade

stem and blossom
cedar and cypress rise in thick copses

apes cry in the mountains
the son of heaven resumes the hunt

the emperor climbs the stone gate
the dead beasts fallen and heaped

confusion strews the bodies
the music can bring no harmony

and goddesses gesture to the gap of exile.

34

what is Caesar's is Caesar's, what is not is not
he washes his feet in the mud

his hat in the clear
trying to avoid drowning.

35

in this country as in that country
they fished through the ice

where human feet would seldom tread

the snow on the river
melon-husk.

36

the lute plays to the moon
visible beyond the window
a goose cries. the wind
bends the branch

the immortals will help me
along this dry road
the vultures hanging in the air
in this long night of fear.

37

the vestiges of men
and women—hearthstones,
wells, ruins—leave at the end
shadows that play at nothing.

five

they are left hoping the past can be escaped
that perhaps we can learn from it

as we run for the hills
the rise and fall

of a dream-space.

                       these dream

sequences sweat now in a row
but are flashbacks too

I spend a third of my life sleeping
and the underground

shakes with that commonplace
in no particular direction.

38

he had a poisoned wound
the physicians could not cure

he sent from Brittany to Cornwall
for her to come and heal him:
the messenger delivered the ring,
but as she neared the port

his wife told him
the white sail was black,

and so turned the sign back
on itself

finding her lover dead, she kissed him
and died.

they lie by the nave at Tintagel
their breath myth.

39

high in the mountains, Saragossa,
was his place: he sat in the orchard
and wanted to go back to Aix
after the triumph against the soldiers

of Malhoun. and the debate over
the cruelty of Charlemayn was not heard
in that orchard

that same sea brought Columbus
from Genoa
the stern of his ship now leaving
behind those

expelled from their own land.

40

the wind on the sands
leaves her
cheeks as pale as peach skin

her grief a letter she writes
herself, a butterfly
in the west garden.

41

the traces in the distance
are bones in the desert
bodies as broken fetters

to rust in the sun, to crack in the frost
regret a crow that grows hoarse
and deaf in the silence no one hears.

42

here are some thoughts
I wrote in Greek on the borders
in wars against the barbarians:
your mind is the habit of your thoughts

in rain and sun, the wind
on this frontier
is cold, but the world
cannot touch the soul

the mind turns barriers
to its purpose.
all lives are but three
of five acts: we pass

into this world, made
and unmade beyond.

43

my father has always loved
those meditations

I remember
the men hauling scrap
with canvas bands on their foreheads

pulling in unison and in rhythm
the wagon while beside them
the great limousine idled.

44

there is a gap in time
between then and now

my tongue strange
their land strong
in my bones

the spring willow
bends on the strand
dreams, not words,
follow now.

45

my guts hurled in the park
the bus ride had been packed
and lurching, the red panda
chewing bamboo like oblivion

and the latrine

grail and silk seemed distant
other images burned in my mind.

46

dreams pursue your gold saddle
my lute knows the sweetness
my heart cannot speak
your lips are no custom.

six

that soldier's eyes are like those
described almost two thousand years

before. barbarity has its own typology
and peace flees like a commentary.

Einstein asked for a new way of thinking
and we lie trapped in our own ambush

the violent stupidity of people in hoards
or hiding behind orders
leads us too close to our own massacre

the killing has to stop.

47

weary on the stern
grim the spirit on the sea

men strive for glory

the ship bearing the weight
of the dead leader

drifts north under roof-cloud.

48

the heart is a distance
truth lives in the birds
and mountains

but words fail
the horizon

clay soldiers
or a Pharaoh buried
far from here.

49

I wed a captain
on this river
he who sails

and seeks a haven

as you leave tomorrow
when you arrive
today: I dreamt

across the waves

I went when darkness
fell and the wind ran mad

eastward to a garden

they swim in unison
among the reeds
as on a painted screen:

my face was once

before
the wind and waters
of my grief—travelling man,

why did I wed you?

50

white blossoms hung

in the wind
beyond the window
as we looked out

at the edge of the boreal

forest in this city
so far from
her home

across the straits from Taiwan.

51

and being in Shanghai
he is better situated
to make his way

in the landscape

and script, although
the ghosts of the horses
with golden bridles

in the south garden

will haunt us both
the Three Sisters,

unable to hold back the flood.

52

a man in France was so sick
he could only crawl: he fell
asleep by a road and dreamt

he was at Saint Olaf's church
in London: there you will be
cured, someone said

as he turned, his companion had
vanished.

53

its weapons were a field of broken ice.

the Norwegians broke rank
to pursue the English, who turned
on them, and, no matter

how great Harald fought two-handed

as he moved
forward, an arrow struck his throat
the wind on the moors shaking the flesh.

54

and in the wind
beyond my garden

as the fields and leaves
shake, I can
read to the ends of the universe.

55

a poem is not silk
but is

thoughts are not silk scarves
but are

the peach tree is a silkworm
silkworms need quiet

poems live by rivers, too
and lines travel.

seven

dreams are inconvenient
are allegories of ignorance

they feel right and real
until the waking, but even then

the feeling persists that the keys
to sleep are more actual.

56

this grief is a cypress
the northern land grows desolate.

57

life is lightning
five-fold hotter than

the sun: it travels
up and down

at the speed of light
faster than the bird

through the mead-hall
far beyond the western end

of the silk road.

58

their shoulders were chariot axles
that rubbed and broke in the closeness

of war. moats and walls were dug
and built: they placed magnets

at the mountain passes to draw
the arrows of the foe.

wind and rain lash

the marble, bramble overgrows
the road

                              music
once drifted over the river.

59

William the Bastard felt that Harold
had taken the English throne

and had insulted him by breaking
the marriage agreement with his daughter.

he invaded and plundered England
tall and strong but cruel, shrewd

and untrustworthy, according
to the Icelandic poet.

Harold let Harald's son, Olaf,
go home with the survivors

on twenty-four of three hundred ships.
Harold marched to Hastings

and, nineteen days after Harald's death,
Harold died, the shaft of an arrow

piercing his eye.
                          most of the English

died there, but Earl Waltheof escaped
and burned a hundred Norman knights

in a wood as another Icelandic poet
in Waltheof's retinue reports:

poets have been part of war
their words invisible swords in the night.

60

the shadow is a body
and is not

the wind rustles
through pines

the bones

feel no pain
under the stones

berries tart
on the tongue.

61

Cathay was in Columbus' head

even as I drift
there among the signs

I cannot read them
and take the unread map

of my blood, tongue, culture
in a dream I do not understand.

62

William conquered England
and wrote about a dream:

Siva said that everyday
when the young boy awakens

he will find one hundred
thousand pieces of gold

under his pillow

perspective is all

so what did the women
think of the dream?

63

in Kashmir the poet said:

he killed his wife as she lay in his arms
and stole her ornaments and returned

to the company of those he would not flee:
the wind was hot and the day was long.

64

naked in the wind
you burn as Babylon
idols in ruin.

65

the sun
greens the hills

the branches are light
that pardons dark thoughts.

eight

the court reports are as strange as any old
archive: lovers do not need scandal sheets

entertainment newsflashes, hotflashes
to say that Freud dreamed of sex

or its typology, which took the fun
out of it and Jung made the unconscious

collective, a kind of group sex
among the symbols.

66

a thief
saw her sneak out and wanted her

jewels and so followed her

she found her lover
hanging from a tree.
the city guard had taken him
for a thief.

                     a vetala in the body
bit her and she fled

at home
she called out:

                  my husband
is possessed

                the thief,
who had followed her all the while,
slipped out.

                 the king did not
believe the husband
and ordered his execution:

the thief told the king the truth
and the king made him a magistrate.

and how wise was the king?
the corpse was laughing by the tree.

67

those not born will have little pity
for any of us

none of the thousand knights
is now remembered

none of us now will have names
those lips will speak

the sleeves of the dancers are boughs
that dazzle and shake

the song dropped
from the clouds.

68

the cloud is a rag
by the moon

the women play lutes
in the vacant woods

the stream cleans
his heart

the wind dusts
her face

and he, on his way
to exile, looks

behind, and hopes
for pardon.

69

the meaning flees
the worlds

words are not
quite

the hand is not
an axe.

70

life fleets
the yields are past

form and matter
cease.

71

my senses are stranded
truth is a line in a maze.

72

the space between tongue
and leaf

shadow
between mist and rain.

73

and the son of Blasine
stands by the king

by the table: the wind
in the dust
is yet a dream.

74

she dreamt she bore a falcon
and saw two eagles tear it

as she looked on: her mother
read the dream for her

as an allegory for a man
taken from her

she kept from men
until her wedding

and afterwards her kinsman
made true her mother's words

and many a mother's child
lay in the path of slaughter

the earth wasted.

75

what are these dreams
that make a language
of their own, fuse

images with a time
not of the day?

this dream salvage
the taste of shade in day.

76

the moon is on the mountain
your lute plays with the quiet

of the world.

77

last night I dreamt
that two boars chased you

till your blood dyed the flowers
on the heath

he left for the hunt across the Rhine
and came to their lodge on an island

on a river: he killed tusker, wisent
aurochs, buck, and boar

he wore a black silk surcoat
and a sable hat

he used his sword to dispatch a bear
who wandered into the kitchen
like a comedy

they ate without wine
and they drew this hunter to a spring

there the king drank first
the water cool and sweet

he trapped him
pierced his heart with a spear

he cursed and scorned them as he died
the shield they lay him on
was red and gold

the murderer devised a story
and the woman,

who had made the Icelandic queen
so full of sorrow, wept.

nine

refuge or salvage, who keeps
the logic, missed logic of dream

straight? analogy and poetry
try to make sense of the cacophony

of night-thrashing, the outlaw,
the beyond the pale, a taboo

that made the world. But some live awake
as in the heat of desire

the embrace of cruelty, their liberty
dwindling, swelling to a nightmare.

why do these images arise
like a pre-history, or early time

erupting, staging a surprise
baffling the rules of life

and poetry?

78

the houses are quiet
in a game of chess

she sings by a blue door
the dragons sleep

on the autumn river.

79

the wars are over
but the wind

is wistful and may erase
the songs

our ancestors once sung
in the shadows of the gorge.

80

in Iceland, the quarrel
never done. after all
the killing, he sailed
across the English channel

where from Normandy
he set out for absolution.
then as he returned past
Wales and north to home

his ship smashed on the rock
as he landed: it was snowing
an old man greeted him
sailed out on an ancient ship

and did not come back.

81

the curse of the sword keeps us
from the earth

the gorgeous truth it promised
in mother's womb.

82

in the history of breath and bone
in the history of dream, silk road
and Roman road, my fingerprints
are all over the object, my DNA
wrapped about the truth I seek,
fact and myth entwined.

just because I dug for China
as a child on the beach doesn't mean
I'll find it.
            when I read about
Caesar in Gaul,
I wondered about the private lives
of those who fled before him.

83

the dog slobbers on my toes as I write
and she has been dead for years.

84

it's hard to believe
an old historian when the day is young.

85

the art of love
has come and gone

official history, the dream
of Africa at his back

a woman left behind
for an empire

although both would burn
in the end.

86

there on the hill he spoke
in praise of the dead

after that he praised this city
where poverty kept no one

from office, where citizens
were equal before the law:

we love beauty and the mind
we are all our own persons

even Homer falls short in his praise
of the greatness of what we are

these men have died for such a city
they have given their lives to her

and I say this in the bright light
of evidence by which they have made

her splendid. they stood up in glory,
whatever their private lives, and left fear

and fought for their freedom and the city
and were swept away from us. fall in love

with her. the city will pay
for the children of the dead

until they are old enough.

the man who had suffered plague and exile
told this to me in the ruins of a dream.

87

moon-bright the river slopes
as if a winding stair

the moon will not drink
my shadow

what is a wine star anyway?

88

the guard wore turbans
and spoke of the blue sea
we were to seek

but on the shore
white bones were strewn
ghosts who moaned

in the ears of the old.

89

She dreamt four times
that winter and wanted him
to interpret these dreams:

she had killed and more
reading the signs of sleep

all this she told her son
and in the shadow of this truth
she grew old, died and was buried.

90

this story has infinite
shapes.

I sing, not arms and the man,
of Helen restored, but of the epic

of dream that breaks upon our lives
waking and sleeping.

but in my dream I remember
what he

forgot: a widow left across the great water.

91

the philosophers
chasing fireflies in the night by the marsh

these stories I have told dreamt
in the vanishing present.

ten

you have to coax your unconscious
it will get you if you don't

it contains filiations between one massacre
and the next, even separated

by a thousand or two years. but even
the waking approve orders

or shoot infants in their mother's arms
even as she is on a train to Auschwitz.

92

he loved her as she rose from the dust
but when she fell a last time, he wept

he sought another startled from her dreams
but it was her he thought
and in the quiet of the midnight world

they endured in unending sorrow.

93

the cave ice hung like a woman's hair
he listens to the wind playing its strings
the red clay still on his feet

from the eastern gate. paradise
is just around the corner.

94

the moss
the moon and the wind-bells
play on her soul like touch

the stone ladder reaches
beyond the stream
her body is weary

the dark sky faces the terrace
her tongue is a lotus
and she dreams of the wild hills

her eyes open as the moon
taste the water she would drink.

95

The voices of the folkmoot
were lost in the wars

and bore kings
whom churches confirmed

and the Witan in England
were those who appeared

wise to the king:
it's hard at a picnic

on the Ouse to think
beyond the thunder

and the approaching rain:
our children and their friends

laughing and unaware.

96

The bird-smear smudges the epigrams
on the monuments

who said rhyme was powerful?

97

the dead below

are laid in troughs, deep as desire
and in her dream she weeps

the tears too salt to quench
her yearning thirst.

98

the long drawn look

on your face
as you sat amid the pine
by the lake.

I won't throw this
into the lake
and this cup

will have to do.

99

the dragon is dying in the river-ice
the fog drenches our bones
the wolves bay in the hills

but that doesn't matter to you.

100

a young woman brings you wine
and the leaves in the Green Mountains
are on fire over her shoulder

you feel the heat in your marrow

the rise in your skin and blood
and the book before you never closes
her skirt brushing against you

in the wind: she has tears in her eyes.

101

the witch plucks the lute
and the spirits, in pleasure

and anger, play on her face
and you shiver as if ghosts

could make you sneeze.

102

the contention of the clouds
from our window

is a reflection: letters, too,
are a correspondence

and the tree in the garden
needs pruning

but its fruit
is not just an allegory.

103

your lips more than a myth
and you find them more than that

when they ache or bleed or prickle
with frost or kiss

more than a gilded image
or a dream.

104

trying not to lose my footing
I hold the moment like balance

so I won't fall flat
and grow wistful

that I missed now
for then and will be.

This moon-writing
is like gravity in space

it leaves traces but cannot be seen
yet without dream what is all this?

eleven

salvage was an old spelling of savage
and it can be dry, like islands off Boston

the Natives massacred and massacring
playing heathen to the Elect

but dream is wild, the typology of wild
being almost as skewed

as the philosophies of hatred.
how can knowledge love

ways to classify the equal to lesser
the neighbour to scapegoat

somehow unlikely images
not so recent, not the obvious

films, books popular in the post-war
but sagas and histories written at ancient

fronts in a continuous war.
Europe tore itself and the world apart

our parents, grandparents, great-grandparents
were there for the bombs: I saw serial numbers

branded on forearms in my youth
and who is the savage now or ever was?

105

the east and west
out of Africa

but as we do
we can and cannot

their laughter
behind us
knowing not knowing

the animist world of poets
where breath and dust meet.